HAMPTON COURT PALACE

ANDREA MANTEGNA

THE TRIUMPHS OF CAESAR

A sequence of nine paintings in the Royal Collection

Christopher Lloyd
Surveyor of The Queen's Pictures

London: HMSO

First published 1991

ISBN 0 11 290503 X

British Library Cataloguing in Publication Data
A CIP catalogue for this book
is available from the British Library

Design: HMSO Graphic Design, Guy Myles Warren

The colour plates and cover illustrations are reproduced by gracious permission of Her Majesty The Queen

HMSO

HMSO publications are available from:

HMSO Publications Centre
(Mail and telephone orders only)
PO Box 276, London, SW8 5DT
Telephone orders 071-873 9090
General enquiries 071-873 0011
(queuing system in operation for both numbers)

HMSO Bookshops
49 High Holborn, London, WC1V 6HB 071-873 0011 (counter service only)
258 Broad Street, Birmingham, B1 2HE 021-643 3740
Southey House, 33 Wine Street, Bristol, BS1 2BQ (0272) 264306
9–21 Princess Street, Manchester, M60 8AS 061-834 7201
80 Chichester Street, Belfast, BT1 4JY (0232) 238451
71 Lothian Road, Edinburgh, EH3 9AZ 031-228 4181

HMSO's Accredited Agents
(see Yellow Pages)

and through good booksellers

Printed in the United Kingdom for HMSO
Dd 293291 C150 2/91

1 Andrea Mantegna, 1430/1–1506

ANDREA MANTEGNA (fig. 1) was born near Padua in 1430/1, the son of a master-carpenter, and received his initial training from the Paduan artist, Francesco Squarcione. Although not a particularly good painter, Squarcione ran an active workshop with numerous pupils and was a passionate enthusiast for antique art. Mantegna's early works dating from the 1450s include the frescoes, largely destroyed by bombing in 1944, in the Ovetari Chapel of the church of the Eremitani, Padua, and the altarpiece of S. Luke painted for the church of Santa Giustina, Padua, now in the Pinacoteca Brera, Milan. These works reflect the style of the Paduan school, but Mantegna quickly came to terms with developments in Venetian art exemplified by the family workshops of the Vivarini and the Bellini. Indeed, in 1453 he married Nicolosia, the daughter of Jacopo Bellini and the sister of Gentile and Giovanni Bellini. The Tuscan artists working in Padua and Venice during the middle decades of the fifteenth century provided another formative influence; principally the sculptor Donatello, whose high altarpiece for the church of San Antonio (the church known as the Santo) in Padua, dating from 1446–9, governed Mantegna's design of the high altarpiece painted (*c.*1456–9) for the church of San Zeno, Verona.

Apart from the Veneto, Mantegna also worked in Rome (1488–90) for Pope Innocent VIII. Mantua, however, was the main sphere of his activity, where from 1460 until the end of his life, he served as court painter to the Gonzaga family for whom he undertook some major decorative schemes in the Palazzo Ducale, notably the frescoes in the Camera degli Sposi (*c.*1465–74), *The Triumphs of Caesar* (*c.*1485–94), and the Studiolo (*c.*1496–1502) of Isabella d'Este, the wife of Francesco II Gonzaga.

Mantegna's preoccupation with monumentality of form, perspective and foreshortening, combined with his interest in antiquity and archaeology, mark him out as an artist in the vanguard of Italian Renaissance art. Many of his friends were humanist scholars trained in the universities of northern Italy and devoted to the revival of classical art and literature. Mantegna himself formed a collection of antiquities that was visited by Lorenzo de'Medici in 1483 and he was evidently well versed in classical texts.

Mantegna was held in high esteem by his contemporaries even though quite soon after his death his style was sometimes criticised for its intense linearity and dryness of manner, resulting in an impression of severity and hardness. These characteristics were in fact modified and softened at the end of his career in the paintings decorating the Studiolo of Isabella d'Este, for example, *Parnassus* and *The Expulsion of the Vices*, both now in the Musée du Louvre, Paris. *The Triumphs of Caesar* represent a transitional phase in Mantegna's style revealing a more pliant use of line and lyrical sense of movement, most evident in the handling of the draperies. While his portraits did not always please their sitters, the large num-

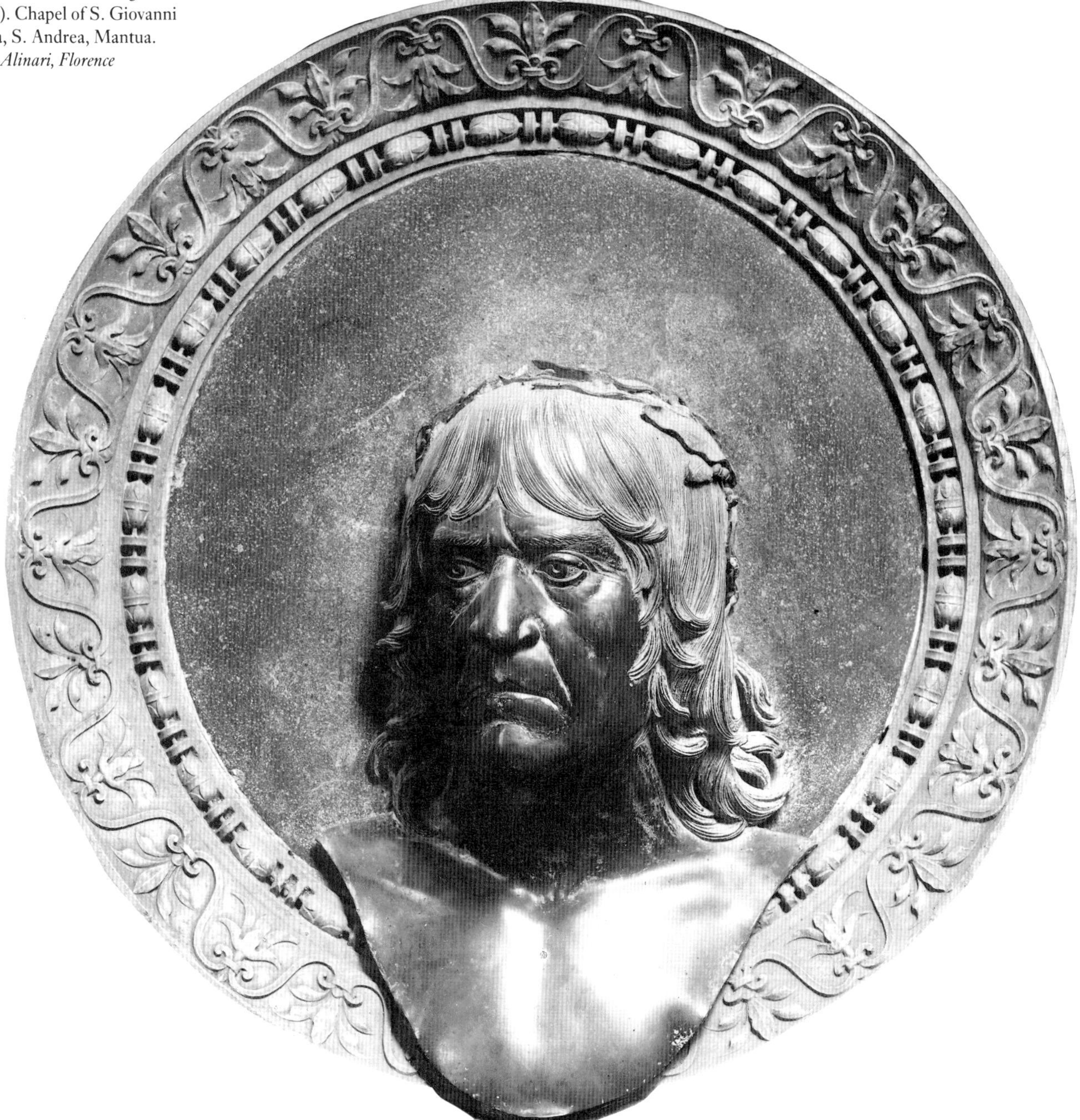

1 Bronze head of Mantegna (*c.*1480). Chapel of S. Giovanni Battista, S. Andrea, Mantua.
Archivi Alinari, Florence

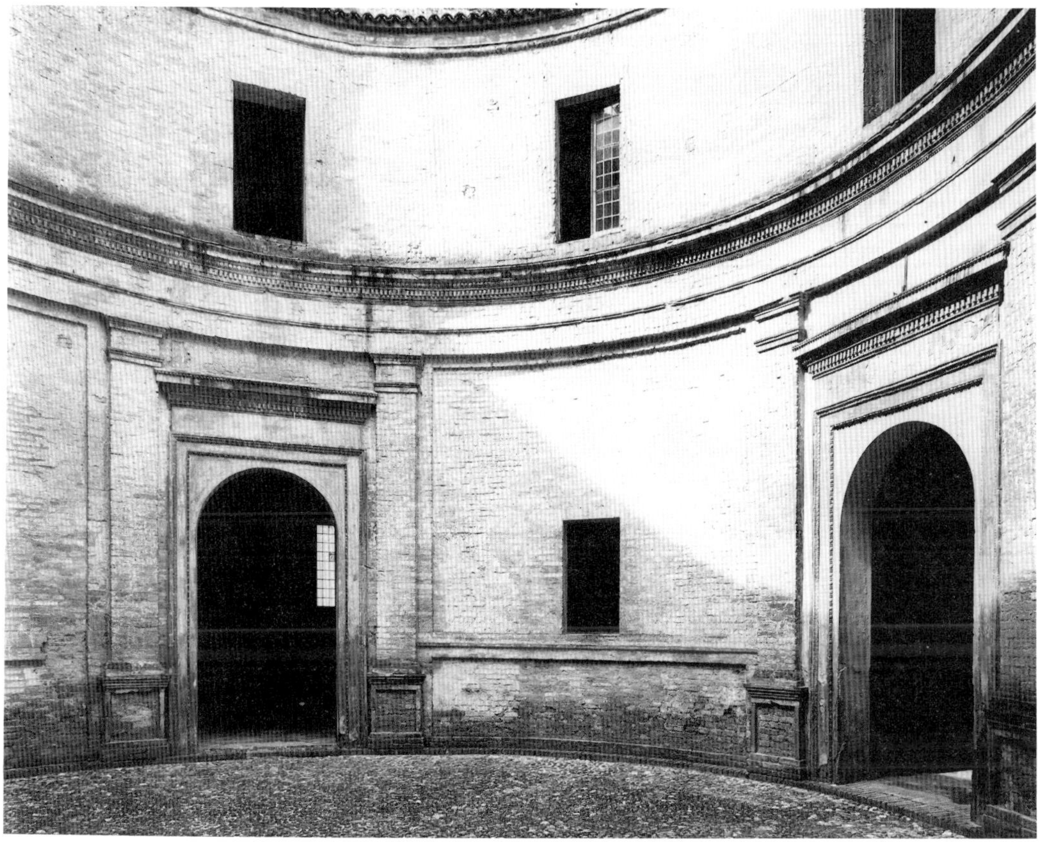

2 Mantegna's house in Mantua.
Foto Giovetti, Mantua

ber of paintings executed in grisaille, imitating marble or bronze reliefs, were much admired. An example, *The Introduction of the Cult of Cybele to Rome*, is in the National Gallery, London.

It is apparent that Mantegna was a slow, methodical worker who often kept important patrons waiting. Documents show that he frequently haggled over money with his employers and conducted his personal affairs in a highly litigious manner. The emphasis on line in his art meant that Mantegna's style translated well into drawings and prints, of which he made several. His graphic work was widely copied even by northern European artists such as Albrecht Dürer. Of all the features of Mantegna's style, however, it was his interest in illusion that proved most influential for sixteenth-century Italian artists such as Raphael and Correggio. Similarly, the manner in which Mantegna was treated by the Gonzaga family anticipates the relationship between artist and patron in later centuries. Evidence of the position Mantegna won for himself in Mantua as court artist are the specially designed house (fig. 2), where he had a studio and space for displaying his collection, and the funerary chapel in the church of S. Andrea where the painter is buried.

2 Mantua

MANTUA is situated in Lombardy approximately half-way between Milan and Venice. The town is located amidst swampy lakes, which in earlier centuries gave it an unhealthy aspect: Petrarch described the persistent fogs and the endless croaking of the frogs, while the dampness undermined the health of the composer Claudio Monteverdi. The background of *The Death of the Virgin* (fig. 3) by Mantegna was most probably inspired by this marshy setting. The economy of Mantua was based on agriculture and the silk industry, but the activities of the court and a vigorous building industry promoted by the Gonzagas provided additional employment during the fifteenth and sixteenth centuries.

Mantua was a place of some military significance during the protracted warfare of fifteenth-century Italy, involving principally Milan, Venice, Florence and Naples. The soldiering skills of the ruling Gonzaga family, who were frequently hired as *condottieri*, could be turned to financial advantage as the balance of power shifted across the north of the peninsula. Similarly, alliances were formed by marriages either to members of other ruling families in Italy such as the Este in Ferrara (Francesco II and Isabella d'Este), or to German families (Lodovico Gonzaga and Barbara of Brandenburg). Throughout the fifteenth century the Gonzagas maintained good relations with their feudal overlords, the Holy Roman Emperors, who sometimes stopped in Mantua on their way to or from Rome. Underlining the political significance of Gonzaga rule and the geographical advantages of Mantua was the decision of Pope Pius II to hold a Council there in 1459–60 for the purpose of launching a crusade (fig. 4). By contrast, as regards the arts and humanism, Mantua failed to develop a local school of painting or sculpture. The Gonzagas strove to attract artistic talent to the town, not just from the Veneto but also from central Italy: Pisanello, Alberti and Mantegna during the fifteenth century; and Giulio Romano, Monteverdi and Rubens during the sixteenth and seventeenth centuries. The climax of this policy was the array of skills that Isabella d'Este tried to enlist for the decoration of her Studiolo in the Palazza Ducale. Although no university was established, Mantua was a centre of learning mainly on account of the teaching of Vittorino de Feltre (1378–1446) (fig. 5). A certain renown also stemmed from the fact that Virgil was born nearby. It is perhaps significant that Shakespeare knew of Mantua by reputation: Giulio Romano is the only Italian painter referred to in the plays and he seems to have known the work of Mantuan poets, while it is possible that in *Hamlet* the play within the play entitled 'The Murder of Gonzago' may have some connection with the ruling family of Mantua.

The Gonzagas seized power from the Bonacolsi in 1328 (fig. 6) and were later raised by the Holy Roman Emperor to the status of Marquis of Mantua in 1433 and Duke of Mantua in 1530. The family established important positions within the Church and gra-

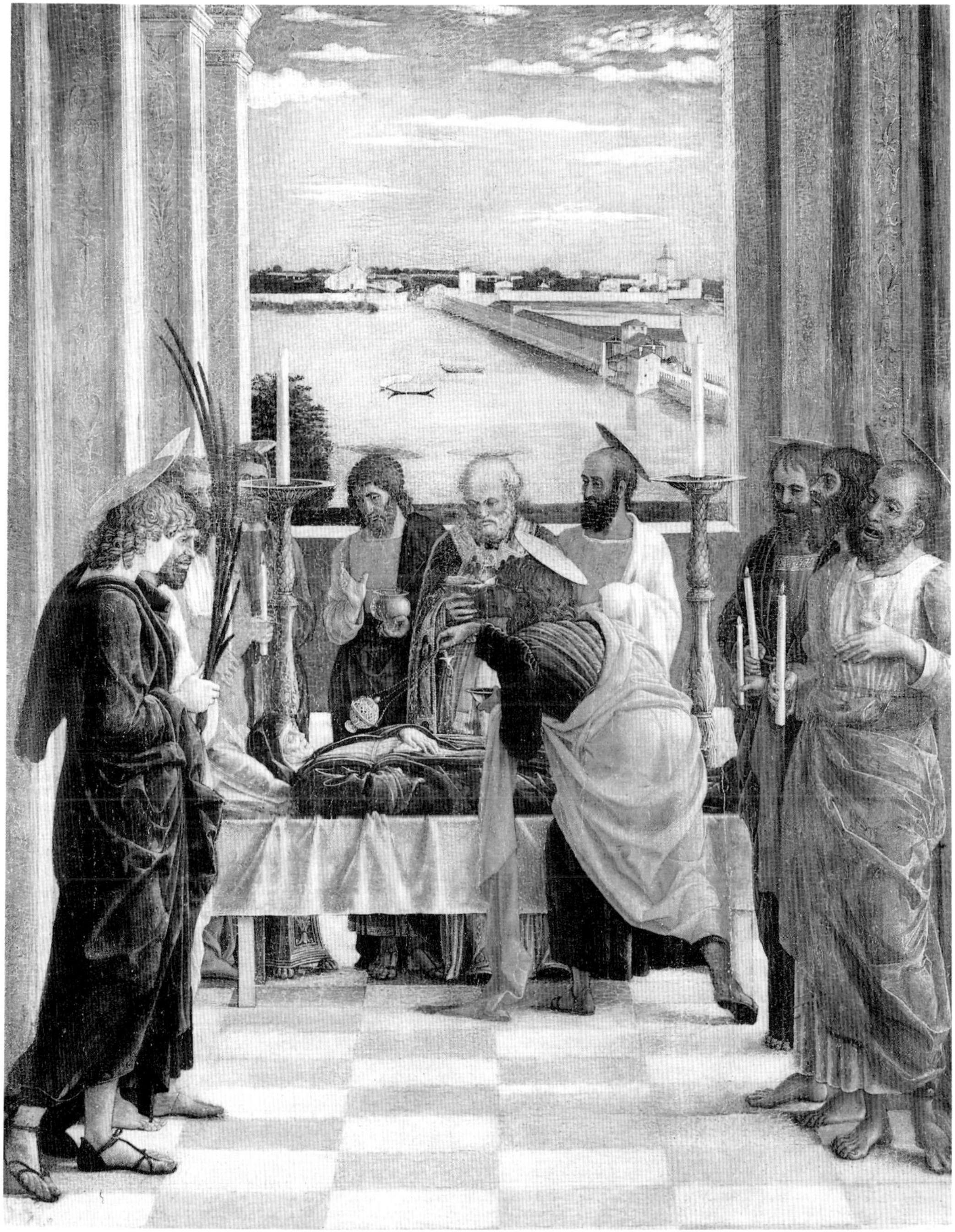

3 Mantegna, *The Death of the Virgin*. Panel (*c.*1465). *Museo del Prado, Madrid*

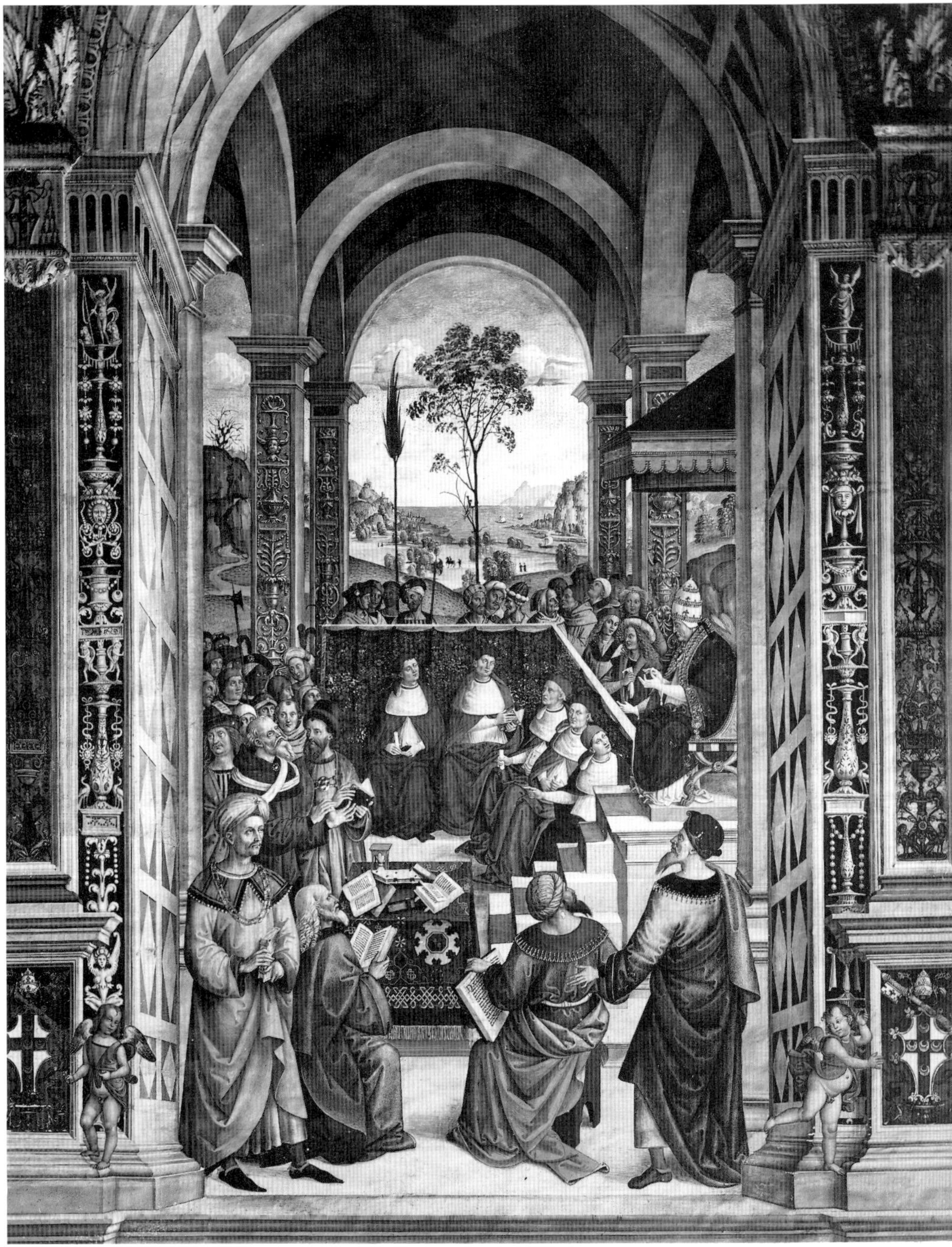

4 Pintoricchio, *Pius II at the Council of Mantua*. Fresco (1503–8). Libreria Piccolomini, Siena. *Archivi Alinari, Florence*

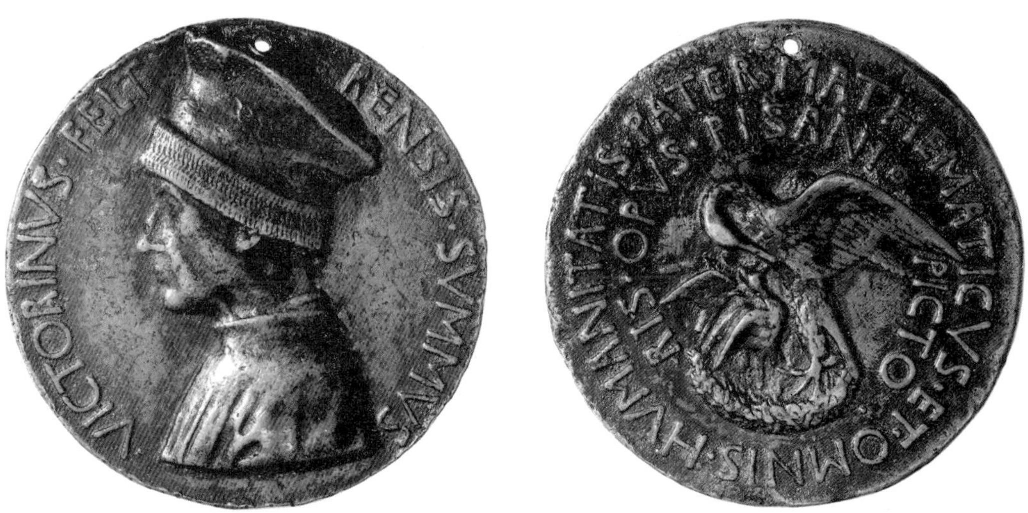

5 Pisanello, *Medal of Vittorino da Feltre* (observe and reverse). Bronze (*c.*1446). *Trustees of the British Museum, London*

6 D Morone, *The Expulsion of the Bonacolsi*. Canvas (1494). Palazzo Ducale, Mantua. *Foto Giovetti, Mantua*

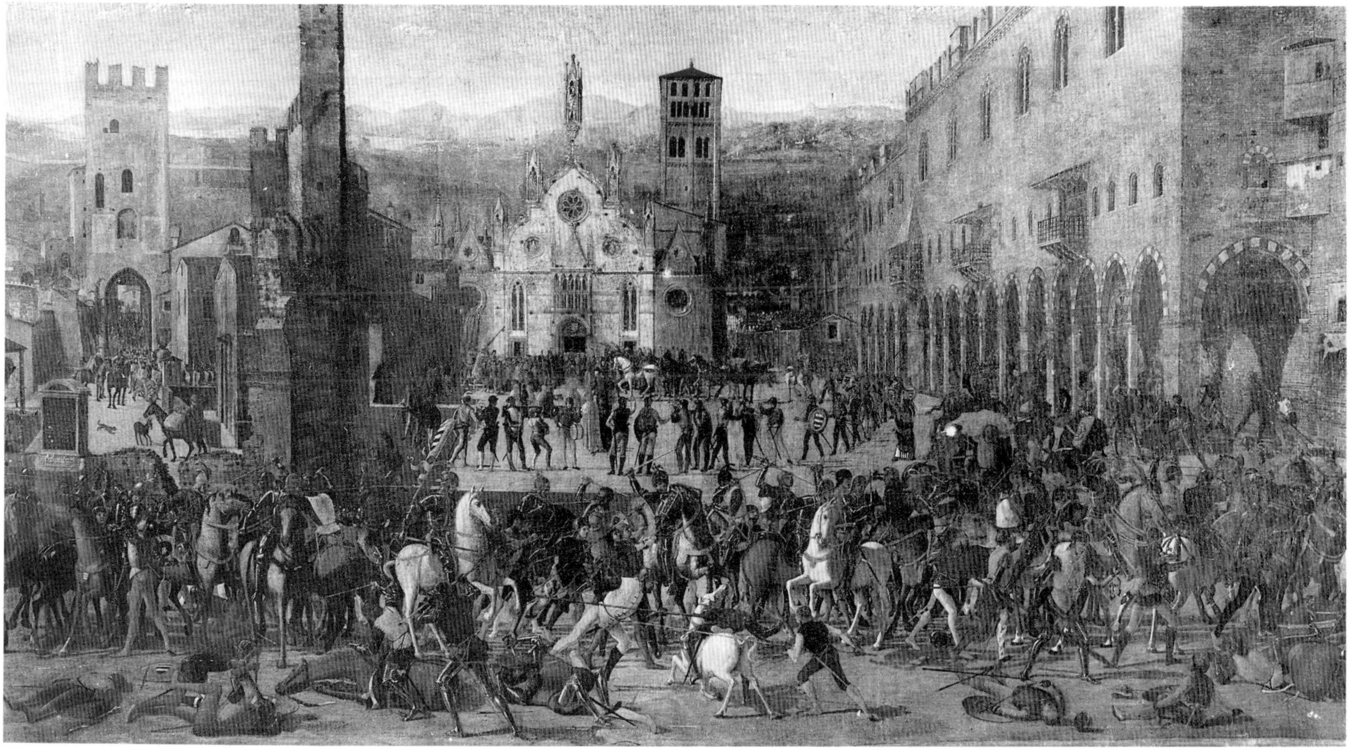

dually during the sixteenth century extended its influence into various principalities surrounding Mantua. However, Gonzaga rule effectively ended in 1627 with the death of Vincenzo II, and the city was sacked by Imperial troops three years later.

Of the Gonzagas, Francesco I (ruled 1388–1407) was a notable soldier and book collector. He set in train the rebuilding of the Palazzo Ducale, first of all developing the range facing the main square (on the right of fig. 6) and then beginning the Castello di S. Giorgio overlooking the lake at the back of the complex. He also rebuilt the facade of the cathedral (see fig. 6). Gianfrancesco I (ruled 1407–1444) invited Vittorino da Feltre and Pisanello to Mantua, but the extent of his patronage is overshadowed by that of his successor, Lodovico (ruled 1444–1478) (fig. 7). Although a distinguished soldier, he also exercised considerable powers of diplomacy. His enthusiasm for the arts, especially architecture, was shared by his wife Barbara of Brandenburg in her encouragement of manuscript illumination (fig. 8). Lodovico modernised Mantua with a policy of architectural and urban development which included the two churches designed by Leon Battista Alberti – S. Andrea and S. Sebastiano – as well as refinements to the Castello di S. Giorgio (fig. 9). It is no coincidence that Lodovico and his successors kept in close contact with Lorenzo de'Medici.

Unlike the Este court at Ferrara, the Gonzagas during these early years exuded a rather cerebral atmosphere. A humanist scholar who had lived in Mantua wrote to Cecilia Gonzaga in 1443:

> In the palace no wanton luxury was permitted: self-restraint was encouraged in all matters of food, of dress, and of habits of life. No parasites or flatterers found a place there, nor was immodest or indecorous amusement permitted.

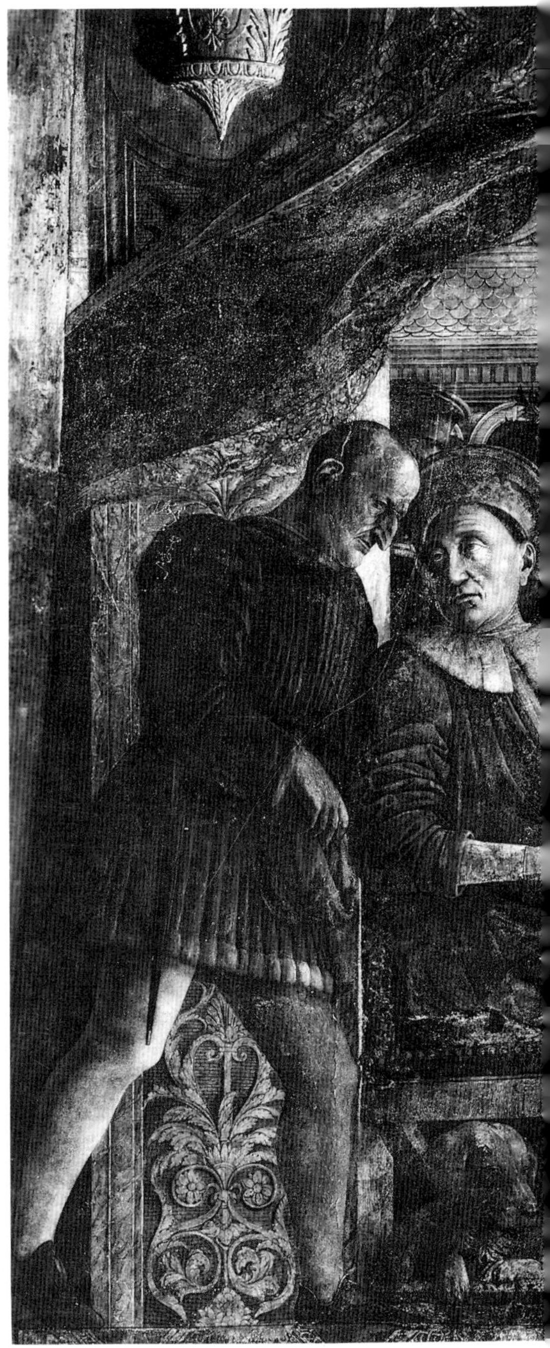

7 Mantegna, *Lodovico Gonzaga and Barbara of Brandenburg with members of their family and Court.* Fresco (*c.*1465–74). Palazzo Ducale (Camera degli Sposi), Mantua. *Archivi Alinari, Florence*

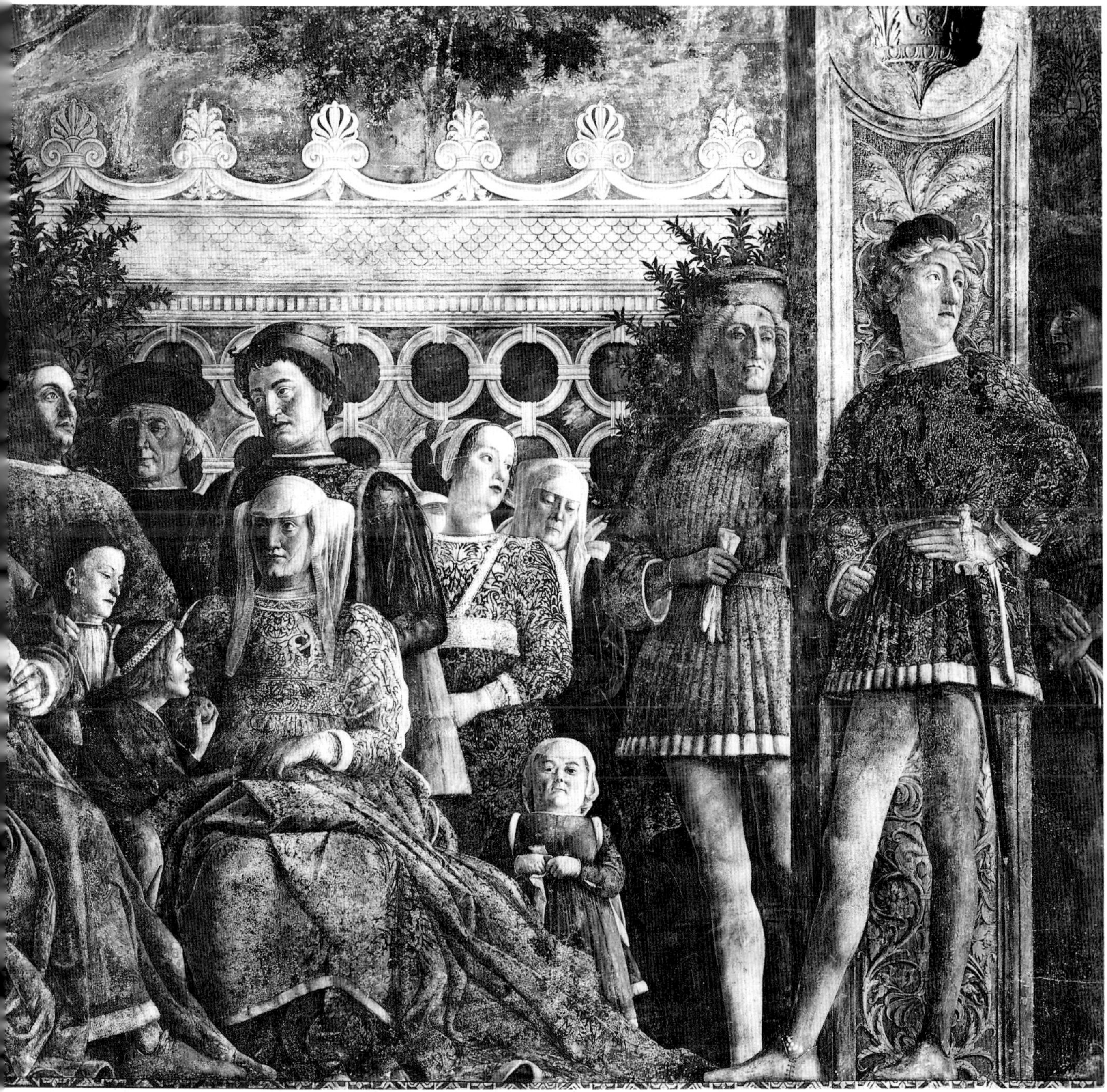

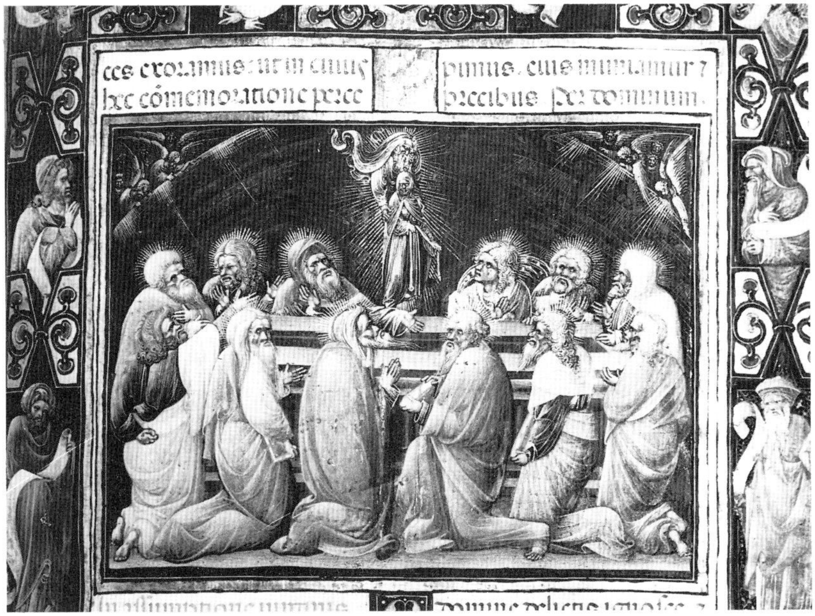

The short marquisate of Federico I (ruled 1478–1484) was marked by the construction of the large Nova Domus by Luca Fancelli, as part of the Palazzo Ducale.

Francesco II (ruled 1484–1519) was primarily a soldier and was famous for leading the Italian league to victory over Charles VIII of France at the battle of Fornovo near Milan in 1495 – a battle commemorated by Mantegna in the *Madonna della Vittoria* (fig. 10). He was not as avid in his love of the arts as his wife Isabella d'Este, but he built the Palazzo di S. Sebastiano and he had a limited interest in pictures and music. Significantly, what is known of his taste in painting suggests that *The Triumphs of Caesar* would have won his admiration.

8 Belbello da Pavia and Girolamo da Cremona, *Illumination from the Missal of Barbara of Brandenburg*. (1450–1500). Duomo, Mantua. *Foto Giovetti, Mantua*

9 View of the Palazzo Ducale, Mantua, showing the Castello di S. Giorgio. *Foto Giovetti, Mantua*

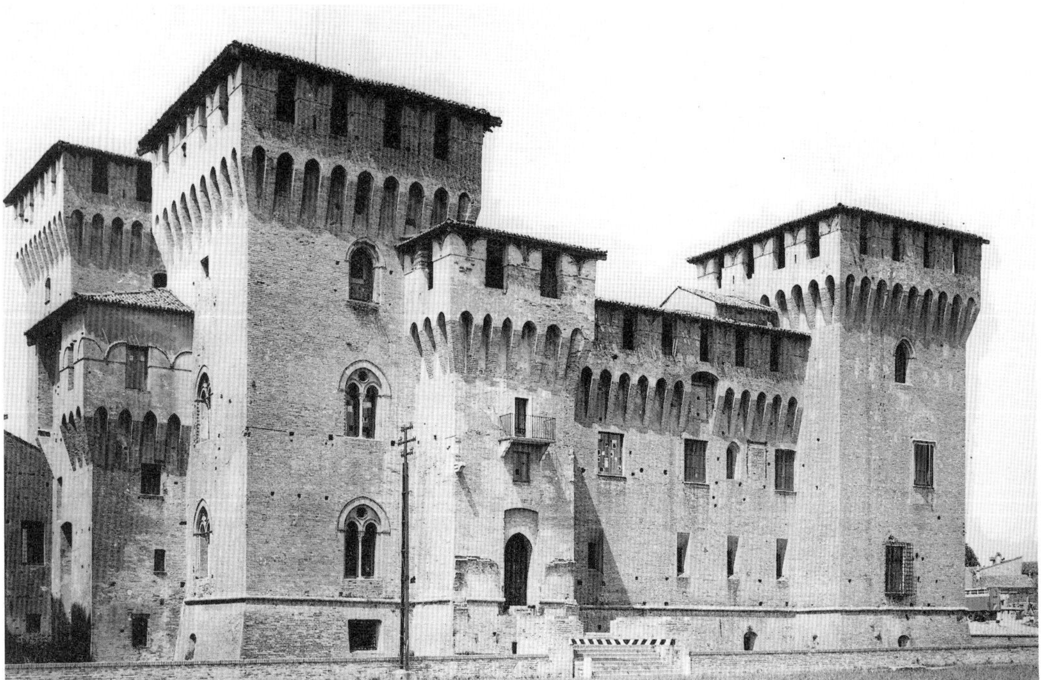

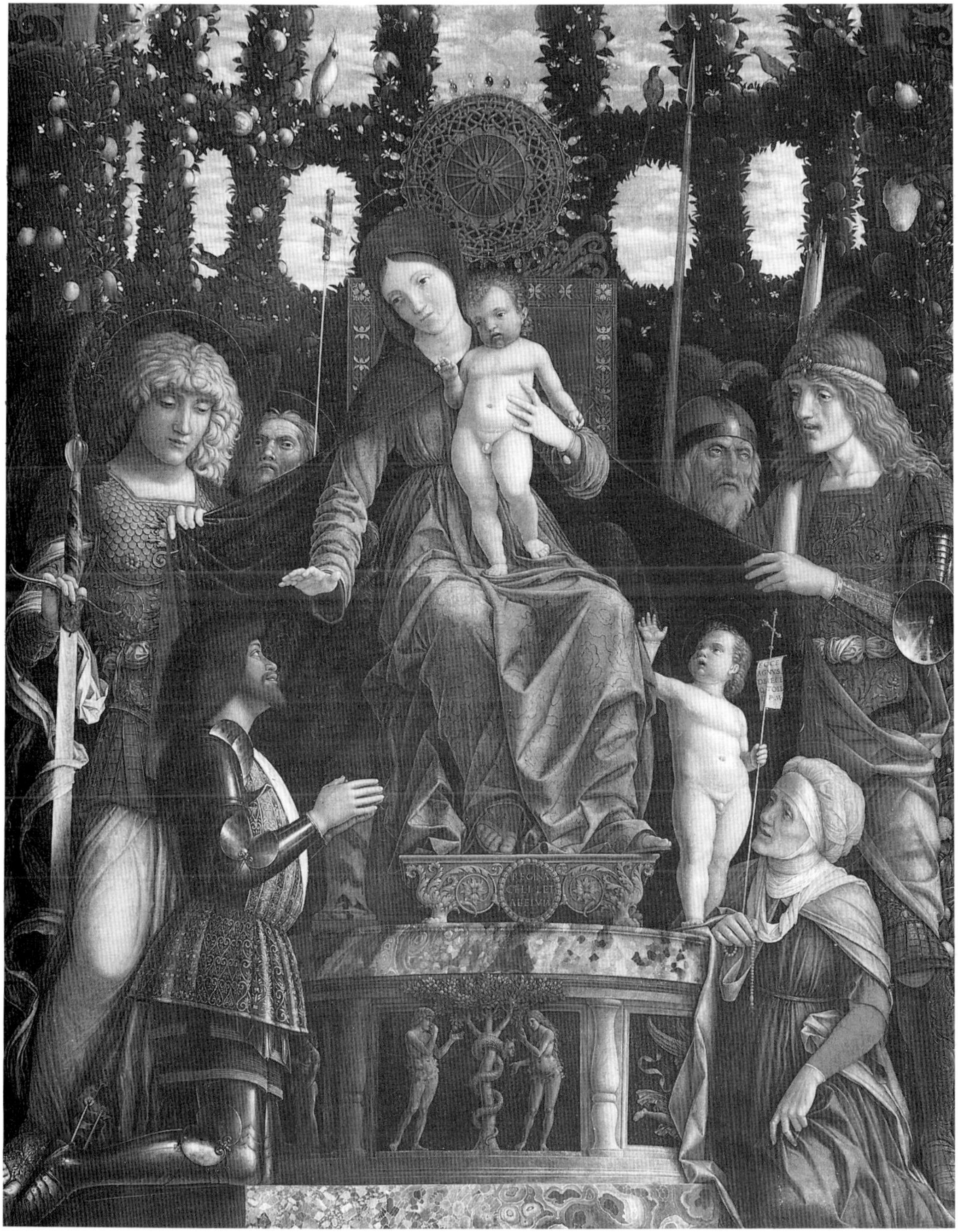

10 Mantegna, *Madonna della Vittoria* (detail). Canvas (*c.*1496). Musée du Louvre, Paris. *Musées Nationaux, Paris*

3 *The Triumphs of Caesar*

THE NINE CANVASES known as *The Triumphs of Caesar* can be counted amongst the finest achievements in Italian Renaissance art. They were much admired during the painter's lifetime, since when their reputation has continued to increase. Giorgio Vasari writing in *The Lives of the Painters, Sculptors and Architects*, 2nd edn, 1568, described Mantegna's paintings as 'the best thing which he ever did', referring to the variety of incidents depicted and the plethora of antique objects represented, all seen from a comparatively low viewpoint emphasising the foreshortening. In each of the scenes, Mantegna successfully fuses his archaeological knowledge of the classical past with his ability to observe everyday life. It is this fusion that enabled the artist to recreate a striking and imaginative evocation of a classical subject that appeals as much by its historical accuracy as by its natural liveliness and invention.

The nine canvases were arguably painted over a period of ten years or so (*c.*1485–94), in all probability for Francesco II Gonzaga (1466–1519) who became 4th Marquis of Mantua in 1484 (fig. 10). The extant documents relating to the project, however, are open to interpretation. As a result, several suggestions have been made as to which member of the Gonzaga family commissioned *The Triumphs of Caesar* and exactly when, and in which order, the canvases were executed.

The paintings, the titles of which are self-explanatory, form a sequence:

- I Standard-bearers
- II Bearers of statues of gods, of an image of a captured city, siege engines, inscribed tablets and trophies
- III Bearers of military trophies and spoils of silver vessels
- IV Bearers of golden vessels and a precious marble vase, the sacrificial oxen and trumpeters
- V Trumpeters, sacrificial oxen and elephants
- VI Bearers of spoils of golden vessels and bearers of trophies and crowns
- VII Captives, buffoons, a soldier and a standard-bearer
- VIII Musicians and standard-bearers
- IX Julius Caesar on his triumphal chariot

The first composition shows trumpeters at the front of the procession with Roman soldiers carrying paintings stretched between poles to form banners. These depict towns and fortresses captured whilst on campaign. The second and third scenes portray an assortment of booty ranging from arms, siege equipment and *colossi* to more precious objects including vases, coins and smaller pieces of sculpture. This theme continues on the fourth canvas, but at this point more trumpeters are introduced and these overlap with the fifth canvas where

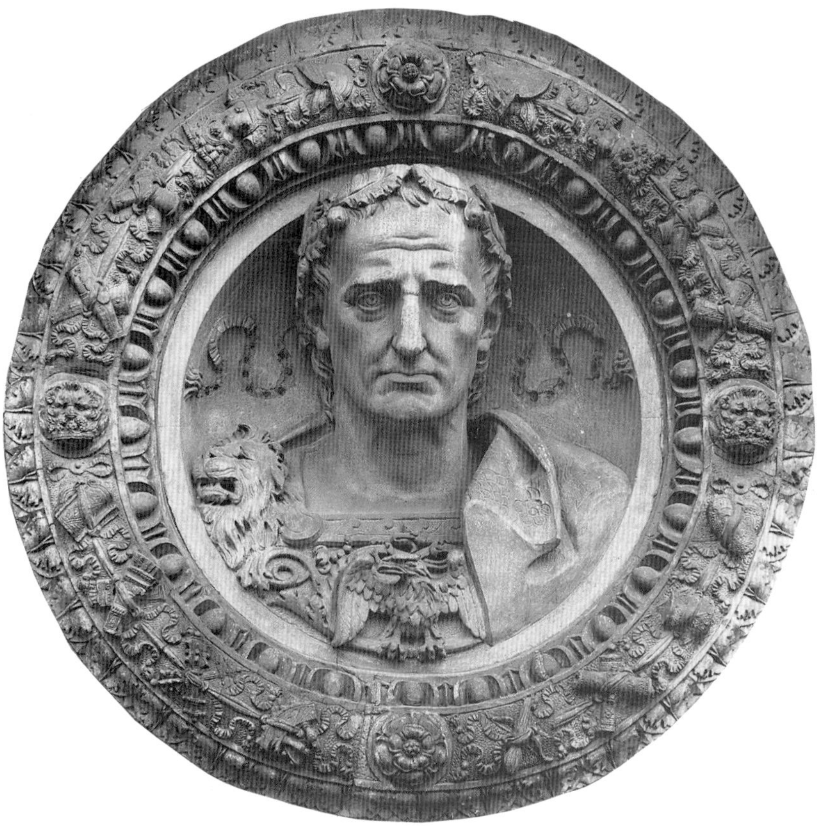

11 Giuliano da Maiano, *Julius Caesar* (roundel). Terracotta (1521). Anne Boleyn's Gateway, Hampton Court Palace.
PSA, London

they are followed by a row of elephants. The sixth canvas has a further array of booty carried by soldiers in front of a walled city. The architectural element is retained for the seventh canvas depicting the captives who are led before the walls of a prison. The climax of the triumph comes in the eighth and ninth canvases. Musicians herald the arrival of Julius Caesar borne on a chariot passing in front of a triumphal arch.

Eight of these scenes are shown at Hampton Court Palace in the correct narrative order, while VII, for reasons of conservation is set apart (*see* chapter 4). Although painted separately, the nine canvases in fact comprise a single subject, namely the triumphs of Julius Caesar (*c.*102–44 BC) for whose military and literary skills there was great enthusiasm during the Renaissance. Indeed, a terracotta roundel with a bust of Caesar decorates the Clock Court side of Anne Boleyn's Gateway at Hampton Court Palace (fig. 11). The visual evidence suggests that Mantegna has conflated two of Caesar's most famous triumphs: one celebrating his victory over the Gauls and the second in recognition of his recovery of the Pontus in Asia Minor. It is not impossible that Mantegna created a composite representation

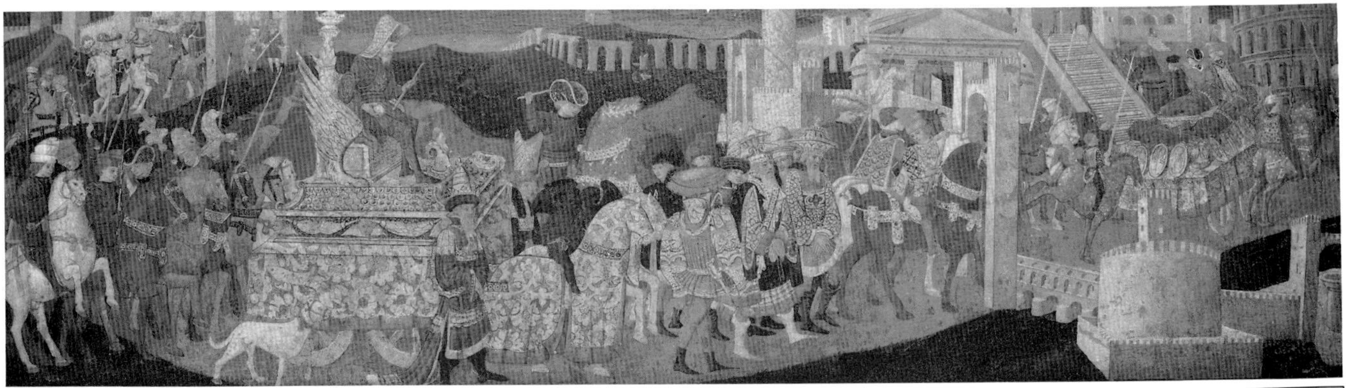

12 Apollonio di Giovanni, *The Triumph of Scipio Africanus*. Cassone panel (*c.*1450). *Fitzwilliam Museum, Cambridge*

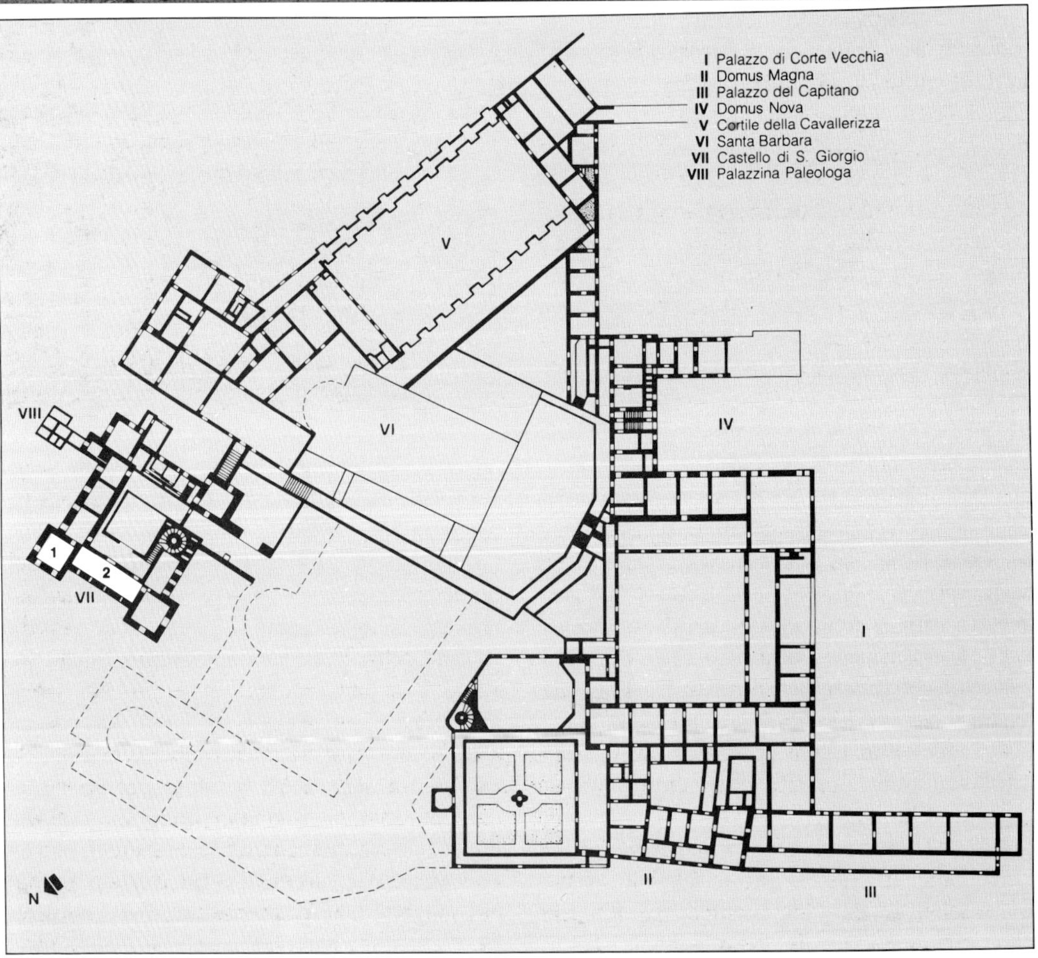

13 Palazzo Ducale, Mantua. Ground plan of upper floor with Camera degli Sposi (1) and adjoining Sala della Esposizione (2) situated in the Castello di Giorgio (VII)

alluding to all five of Caesar's known triumphs. For knowledge of these and comparable events Mantegna could have consulted such writers as Suetonius, *Lives of the Caesars*, Plutarch, *Parallel Lives* and Appian, *Romaica*, all of whom include descriptions of triumphs and were available during the Renaissance in manuscript or printed forms. In addition to literary sources, the artist undoubtedly referred to Roman antiquities, particularly the monumental arches and columns which he would have known through drawn copies collected by his friends such as the antiquarian Giovanni Marcanova. Apart from the collections of antique sculpture, inscriptions, precious stones, coins and medals to which Mantegna had access, he would also have had recourse to contemporary publications including Flavio Biondo, *Roma triumphans*, 1472, and Roberto Valturio, *De re militari*, 1472. Even though Mantegna did visit Rome (1488–90) while working on these canvases, he could have devised the compositions for *The Triumphs of Caesar* before his departure on the basis of his wide knowledge of ancient ruins gained earlier in his life. No doubt the visit to Rome rekindled Mantegna's inspiration, but he was by no means slavishly dependent upon any of the cited sources and there are few direct quotations from known earlier representations. Essentially, *The Triumphs of Caesar* are works of great imaginative force, being no less than a recreation of an ancient Roman tradition based on the latest archaeological research. They are undeniably a considerable advance upon the more conventional depictions of triumphs (fig. 12) usually found on fifteenth-century *cassoni* (marriage chests).

Certain aspects of *The Triumphs of Caesar* remain unclear. Just as the exact date of the commission is not documented, so too the intended location, the arrangement of the paintings and even the order in which they were executed, are open to discussion. It has been suggested that they might have been painted for display in the main *sala* on the second floor of the Palazzo Ducale in Mantua (fig. 13) adjoining the Camera degli Sposi, decorated by Mantegna at an earlier date in fresco. The paintings were most probably preceded by detailed compositional drawings, some of which are known from engravings. A related drawing in Vienna (fig. 14) shows a scene of senators walking in procession following the triumphal chariot conveying Caesar. This was not apparently executed as a painting and suggests that Mantegna failed to complete the full sequence of planned scenes. He might,

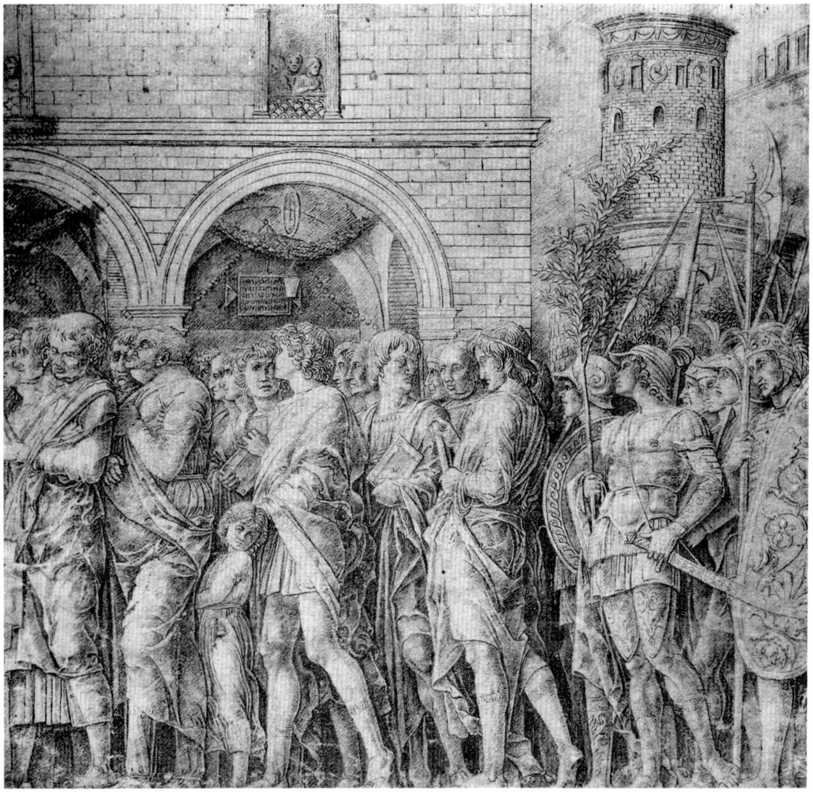

14 Mantegna (*after*), *The Senators*. Drawing. Pen and brown ink. *Fonds Albertina, Vienna*

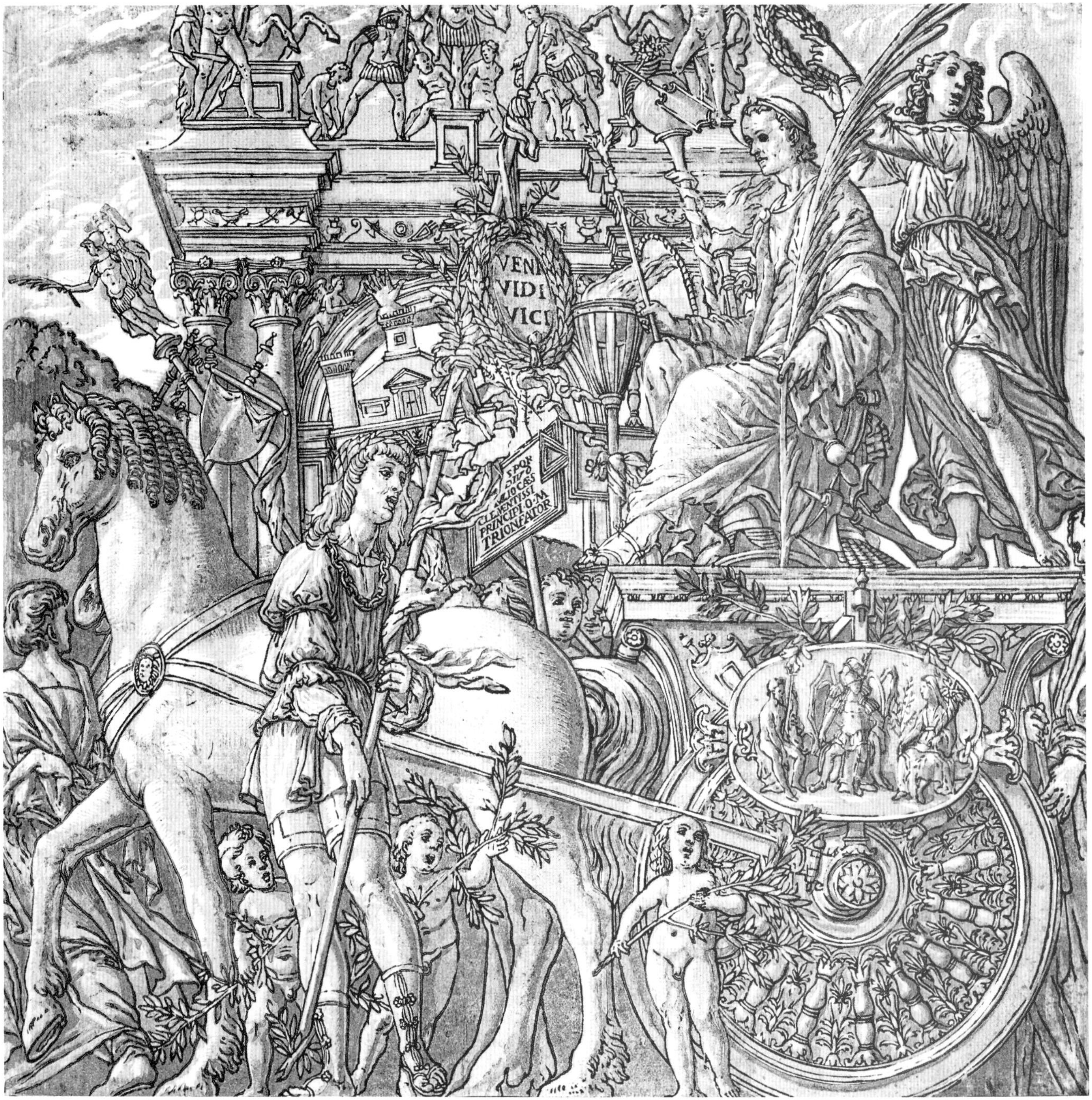
VENI
VIDI
VICI
S.P.Q.R.
DIVO
CAES
PRINCIPI.O.M
TRIONFATOR

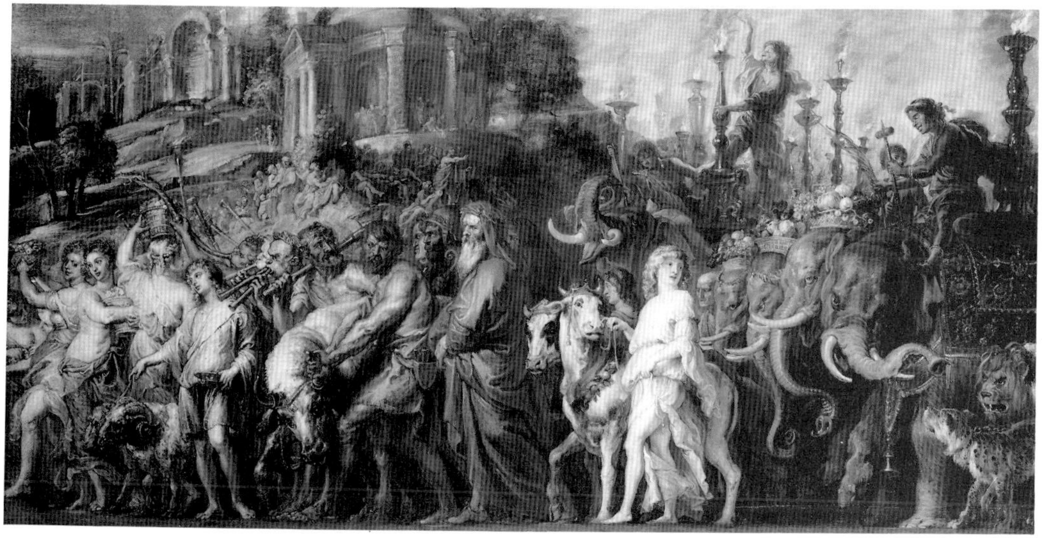

15 Andrea Andreani, *The Triumphs of Caesar* (canvas IX). Chiaroscuro woodcut (1599). *Trustees of the British Museum, London*

16 Rubens, *A Roman Triumph*. Canvas laid on panel (*c.*1628). *National Gallery, London*

therefore, have been encouraged by Francesco II Gonzaga to compress the narrative, or even curtail work on individual canvases, in order to bring to a conclusion a commission required for such a public space that had already preoccupied the artist for a number of years. The drawing in Vienna would have followed the ninth canvas and therefore brought the narrative to a close. In theory yet other scenes could have been contemplated. The canvases might have been shown in a line, because Mantegna has used only a single light source illuminating each scene from the left. Alternatively, they could have been distributed around the walls of a room. Since the *sala* in question was oblong and one of its walls was pierced by windows, then, if the whole sequence amounted to ten canvases, two groups of three might have been placed on the short walls with four on the remaining long wall.

In whatever order the canvases were meant to be seen, there can be no doubt that Mantegna conceived them as a group using such devices as compositional continuity, repetition of colour, direction of light and treatment of the backgrounds to unify the narrative. He also intended *The Triumphs of Caesar* to be seen slightly from below. They were divided by pilaster frames so that the viewer would witness the procession as though from within a *loggia* thereby adding to the sense of movement and clamour. It is not at all certain, however, that they were ever permanently installed in the proposed *sala* of the Palazzo Ducale or, indeed, in any other part, and they may only have been used as temporary decoration on special festive occasions. By 1507 the canvases had already been moved to Francesco II's new Palazzo di S. Sebastiano. A number of early painted copies of *The Triumphs of Caesar* on varying scales are known. The first set of prints after the paintings was the series of chiaroscuro woodcuts by Andrea Andreani (1558/9–1629), *Tabulae Triumphi Caesaris* ... published in Mantua in 1599 (fig. 15). Perhaps the most famous emulation of Mantegna's achievement is Ruben's *A Roman Triumph* painted *c.*1628 (fig. 16). Rubens had worked for the Gonzaga family in Mantua during the first decade of the seventeenth century.

17 Andrea Andreani, *The Captives* (canvas VII). Chiaroscuro woodcut (1599). *Trustees of the British Museum, London*

4 *The Triumphs of Caesar* and the Royal Collection

THE TRIUMPHS OF CAESAR were acquired by Charles I in 1629 when he purchased a large part of the collections formed by the Gonzaga family. The purchase also included important works by Titian, Raphael, Correggio, Annibale Carracci, Reni and Caravaggio thus adding considerably to the reputation of Charles I's collection as one of the finest ever formed. *The Triumphs of Caesar* had been much admired in Mantua and were frequently shown to visitors even during Mantegna's lifetime. Daniel Nys, who acted as an agent for Charles I when negotiating firstly with Vincenzo II and then with his successor Carlo I, commented that 'not having *The Triumphs of Caesar*, I had nothing at all'. They were clearly considered to be the masterpiece of the Gonzaga collection and it is significant that Vincenzo II withheld them from sale during the opening negotiations in 1625. The canvases have been hung at Hampton Court Palace since the probable date of their arrival in England in 1630, and tapestries based on some of the scenes were woven at the Mortlake factory – three are in the collection of the Duke of Buccleuch at Bowhill House. The same factory made a set of tapestries based on the Raphael Cartoons, also acquired by Charles I, and for many years shown at Hampton Court Palace – now in the Victoria and Albert Museum.

When Charles I's collection was dispersed following his execution in 1649, *The Triumphs of Caesar* were listed in an inventory at a value of £1,000, but they were reserved from sale and remained at Hampton Court Palace during the Protectorate and thereafter. Until 1689 the paintings were hung in the King's Gallery of the Tudor Palace, but following the rebuilding during the reign of William III and Mary II they were moved to various other parts of the Palace before their installation in the Lower Orangery in 1919.

The Triumphs of Caesar have been restored several times and already in the seventeenth century their condition was giving rise to anxiety. The 'Captives' (VII), for example, was described in 1660 as 'much spoyled'. The nine paintings are executed on a 'twilled' linen canvas prepared with a thin layer of gesso over which tempera has been applied. They are the most extensive surviving group of tempera paintings by a major artist of the Italian Renaissance. The individual canvases each comprise three vertical strips, two broad and one narrow, sewn together. Owing to the gradual deterioration of the paintings, three major campaigns of restoration have been undertaken in an attempt to arrest the process. The first programme of conservation was initiated by Parry Walton (*c.*1690–3) and continued by Louis Laguerre (*c.*1694–1702) and then by Joseph Goupy (1717). The treatment involved relining three of the canvases and extensive, heavy retouching of all nine, which is still partially evident today. This attempt at restoration was disastrous. The second campaign was conducted by Kennedy North between 1931 and 1934. North relined all the canvases and secured the lifting paint

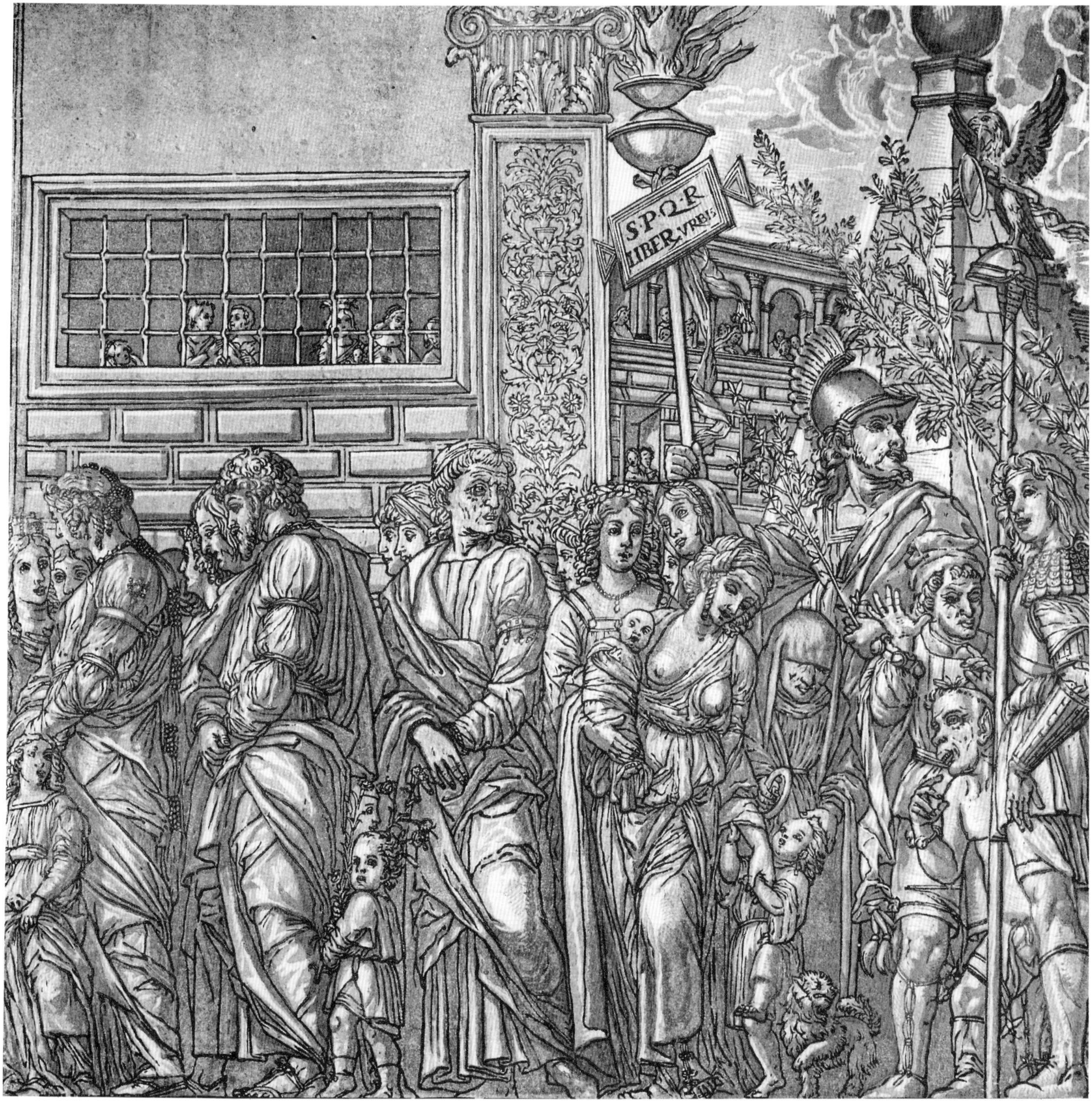
S·P·Q·R
LIBER VRBIS

surface, but his techniques were radical and in the long term unsuccessful. The most effective and sensitive restoration was undertaken by John Brealey between 1962 and 1974. The success of this recent restoration lay in the fact that old repaint was removed and wherever possible Mantegna's original paint revealed. In the case of the 'Captives' (VII) it was found that no original paint lay below the surface and so this was left in an uncleaned state. A clearer impression of this composition can be gained from the chiaroscuro woodcut published by Andrea Andreani in 1599 (fig. 17). It is apparent that *The Triumphs of Caesar* have over the years suffered from damage and heavy retouching. The effects of the glazes have been seriously reduced and the subtlety of the modelling reduced by wear. Yet, owing to the recent restoration, the original impact of the paintings is by no means totally lost so that today it is still possible to agree with Vasari that 'the entire work could not be made more beautiful or improved'.

Further Reading

A Martindale. *The Triumphs of Caesar by Andrea Mantegna in the Collection of Her Majesty The Queen at Hampton Court*. London, 1979.

D Chambers and J Martineau, (eds). *Splendours of the Gonzaga*. Catalogue of an exhibition held in the Victoria and Albert Museum, 1981–2. London, 1981.

R Lightbown. *Mantegna*. Oxford, 1986.

Each of the above has a full bibliography.

THE TRIUMPHS OF CAESAR

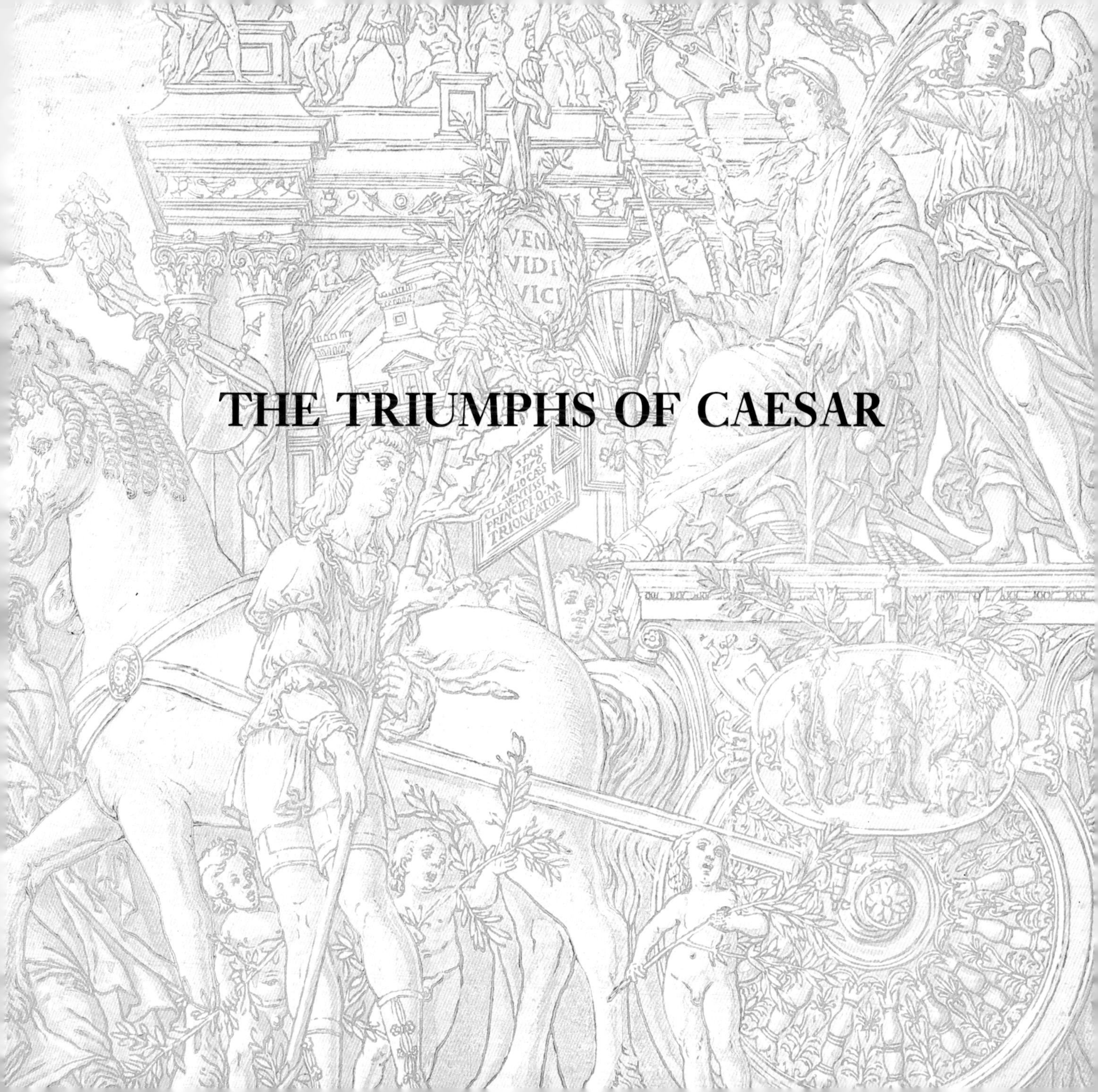

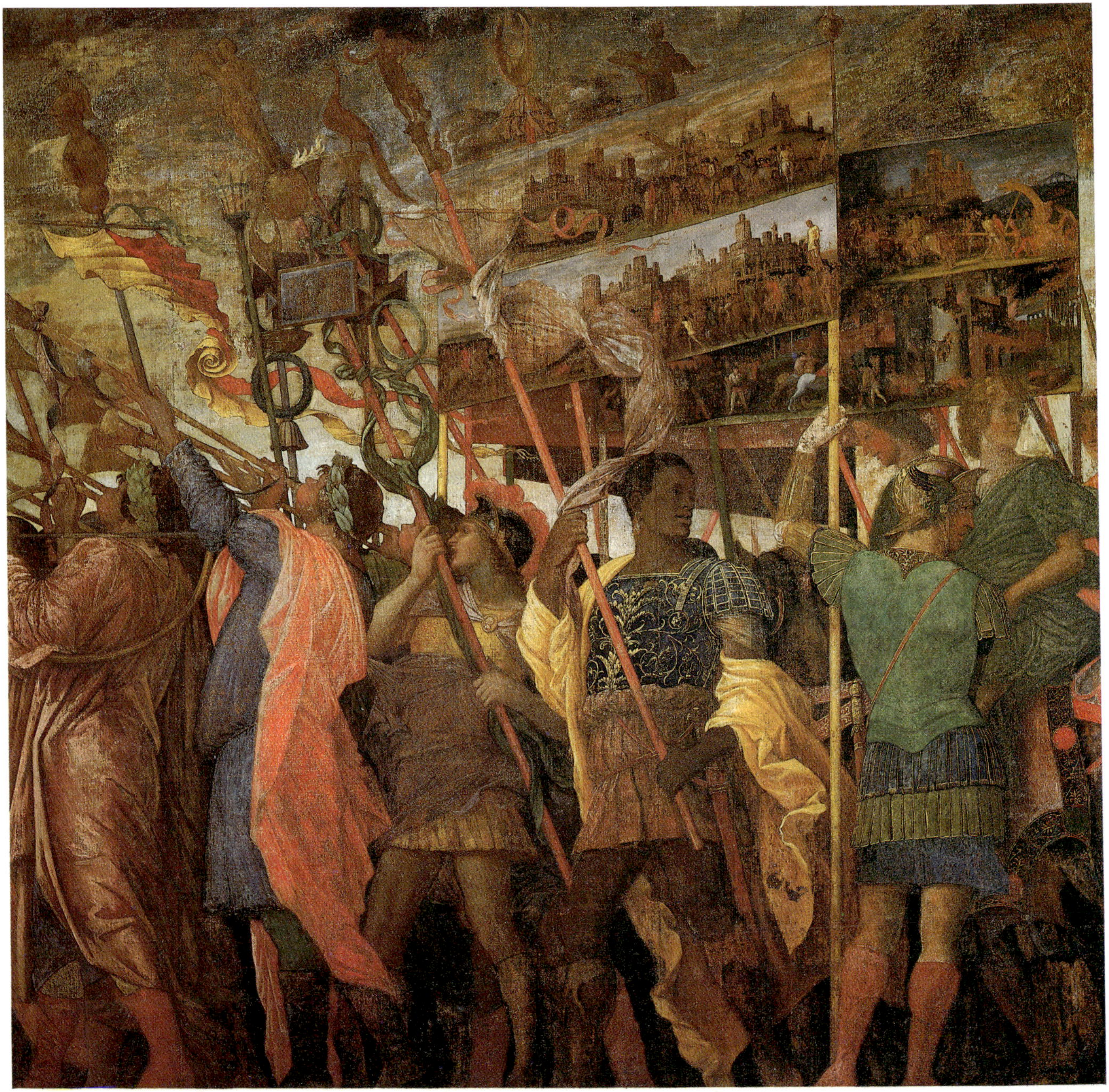

1 Standard-bearers (*canvas I*)

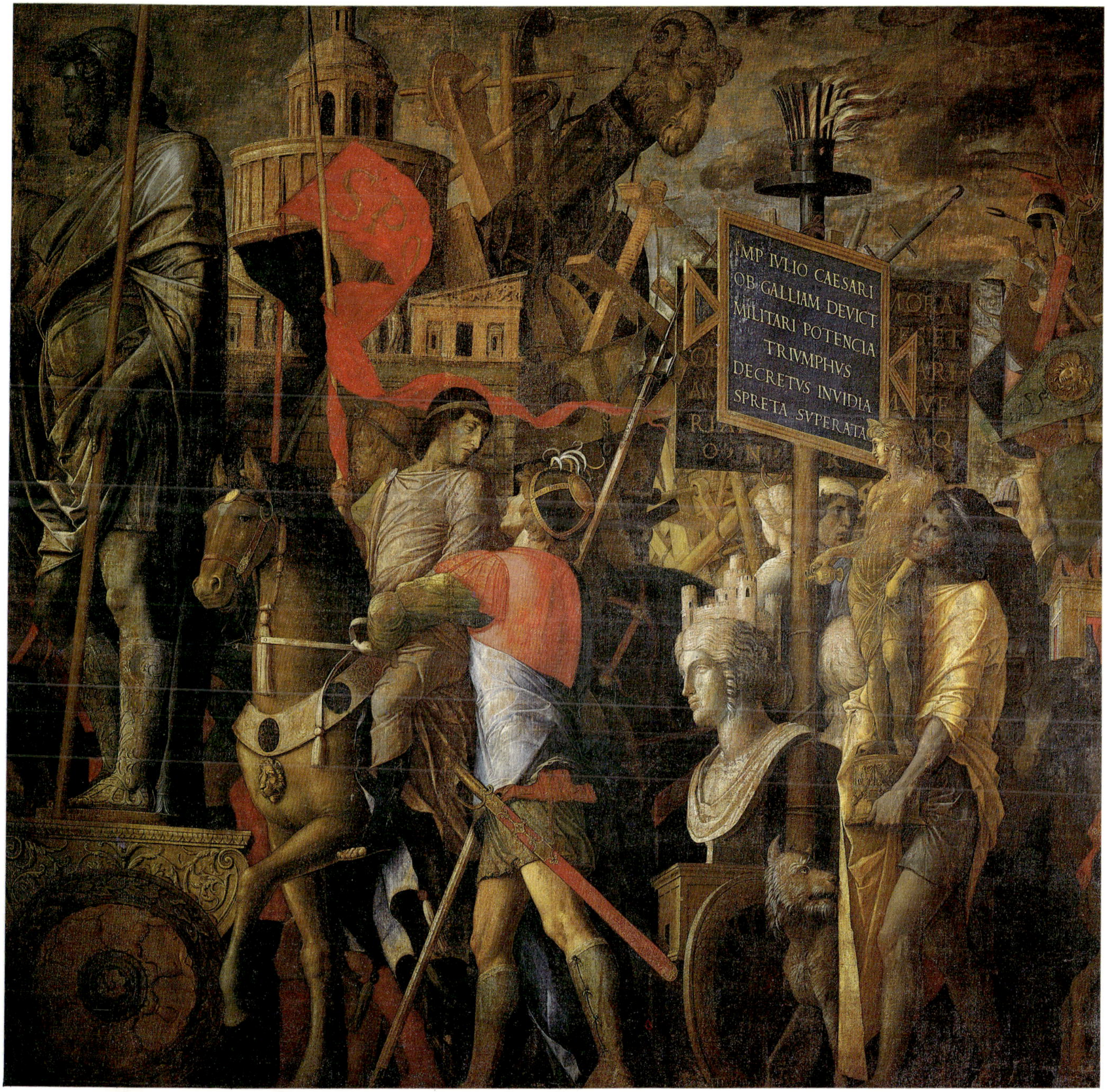

2 Bearers of statues of gods, of an image of a captured city, siege engines, inscribed tablets and trophies (*canvas II*)

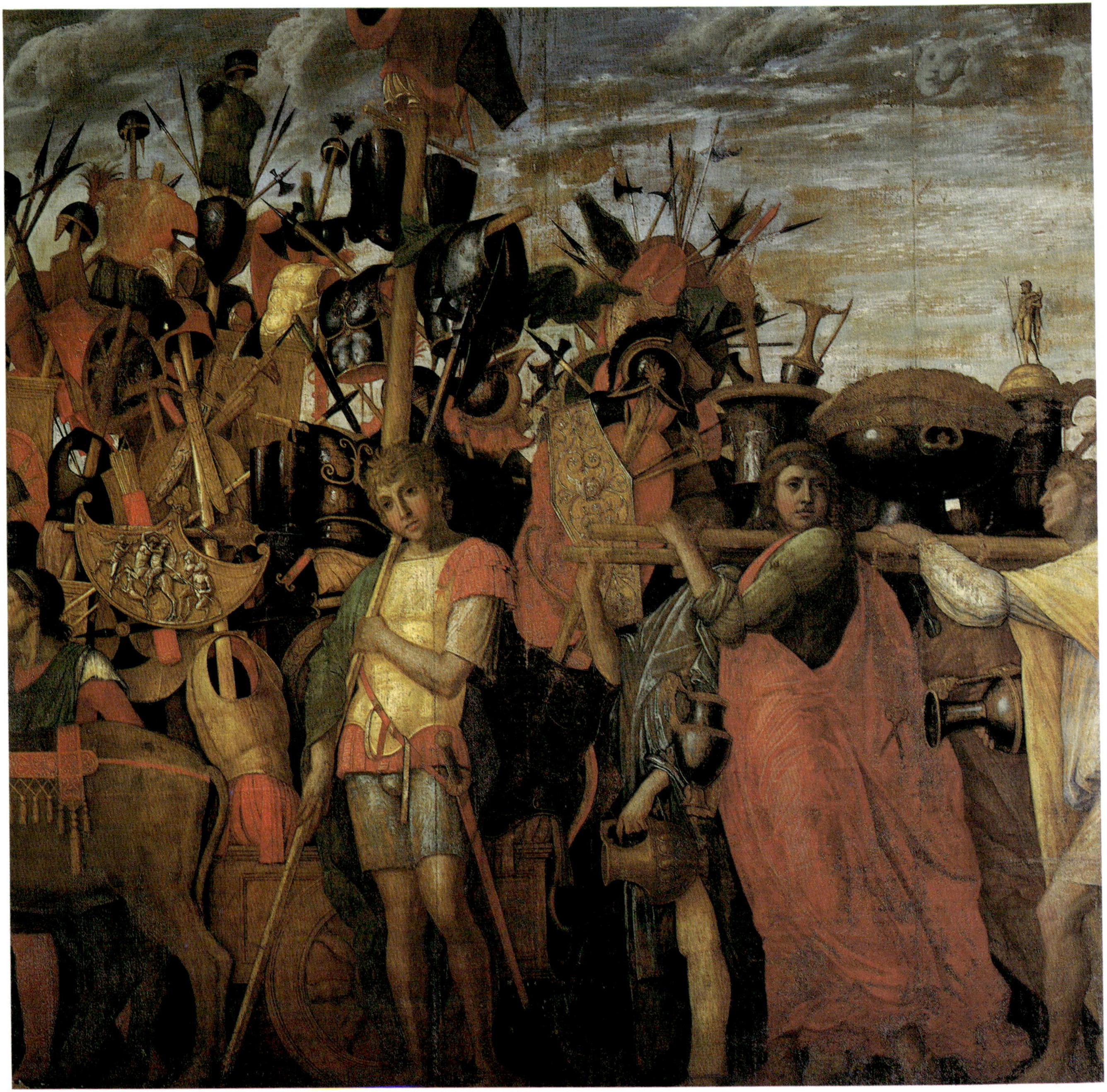

3 Bearers of military trophies and spoils of silver vessels (*canvas III*)

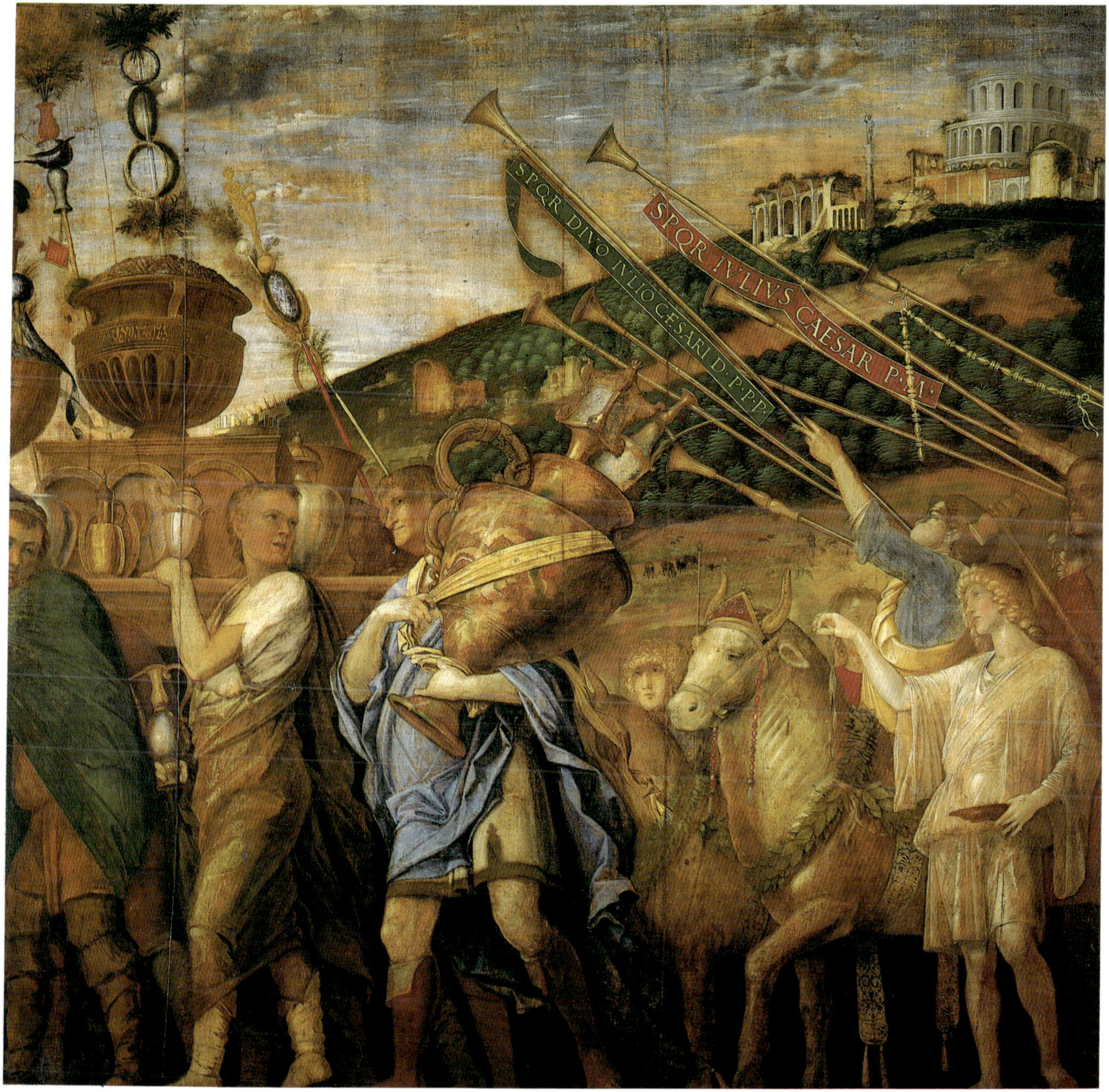

4 Bearers of golden vessels and a precious marble vase, the sacrificial oxen and trumpeters (*canvas IV*)

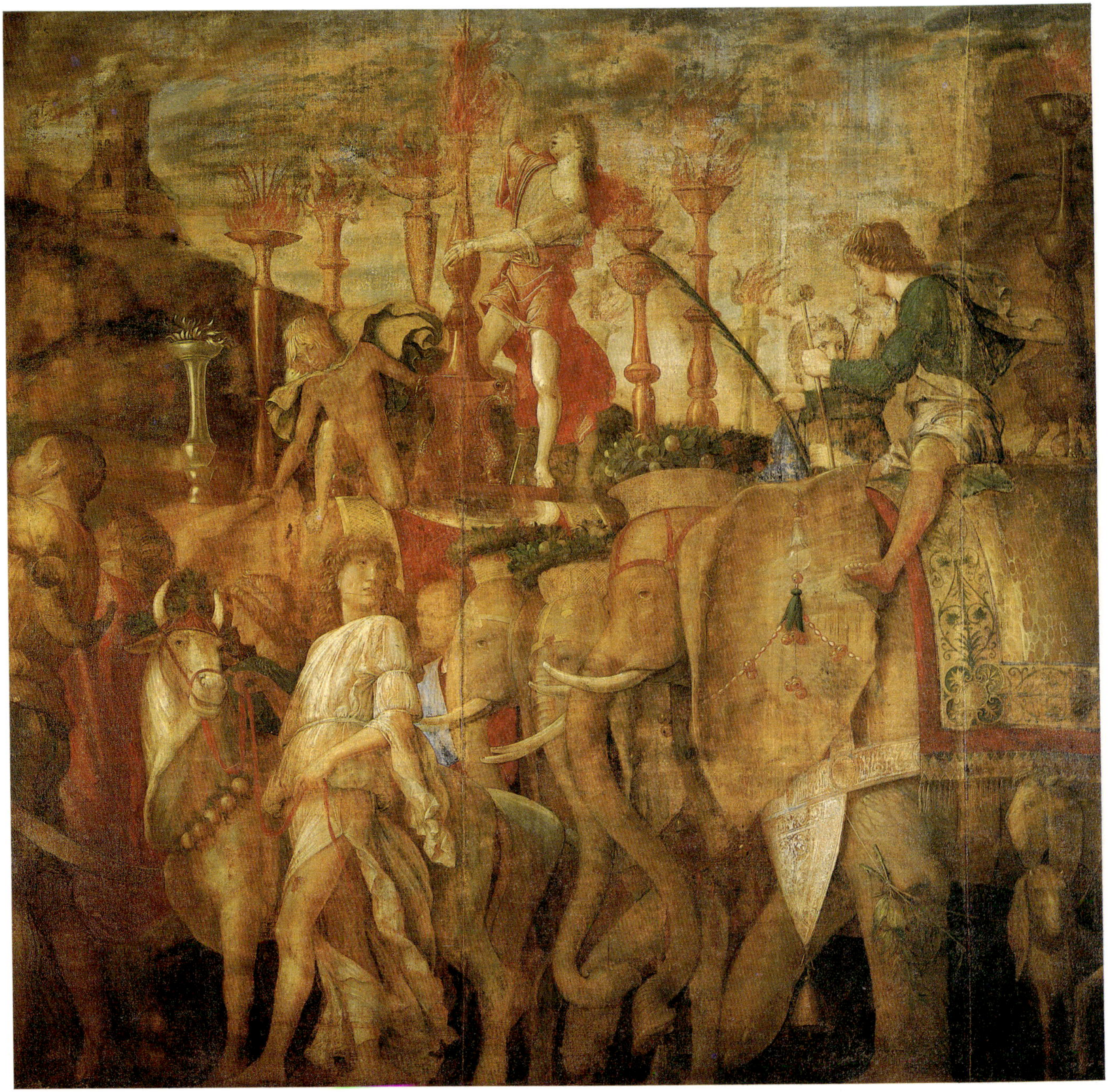

5 Trumpeters, sacrificial oxen and elephants (*canvas V*)

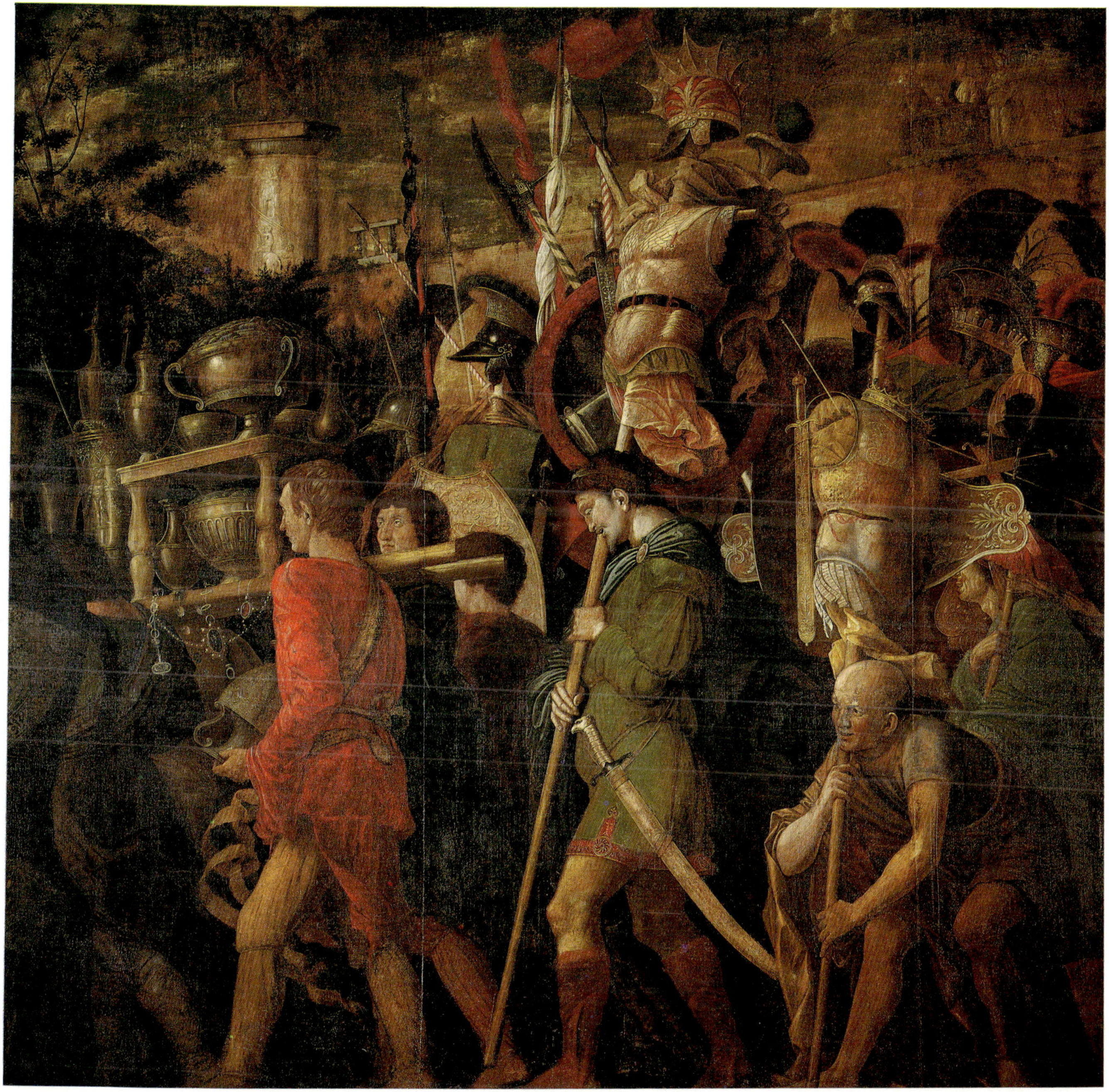

6 Bearers of spoils of golden vessels and bearers of trophies and crowns (*canvas VI*)

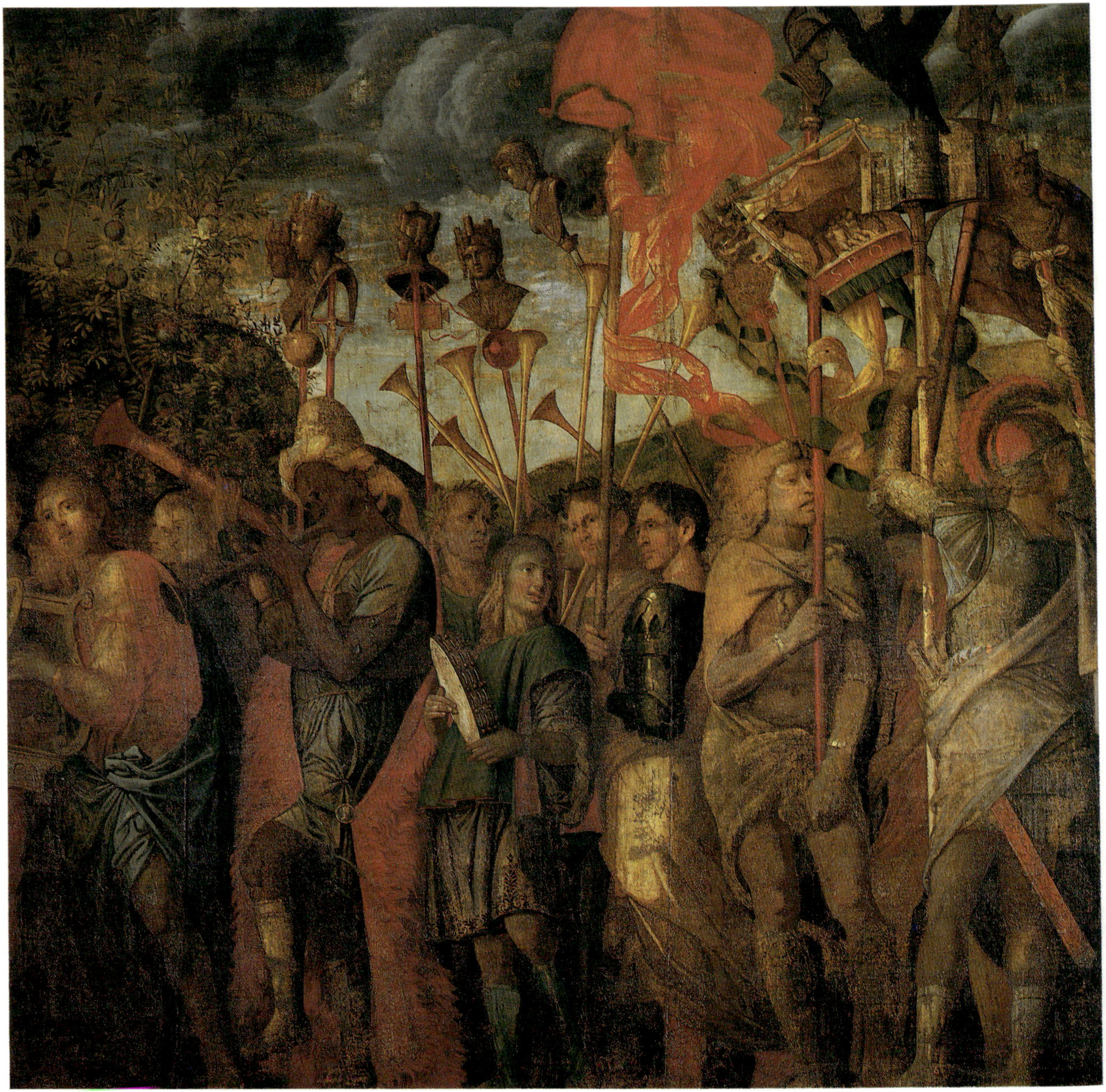

7 Musicians and standard-bearers (*canvas VIII*)

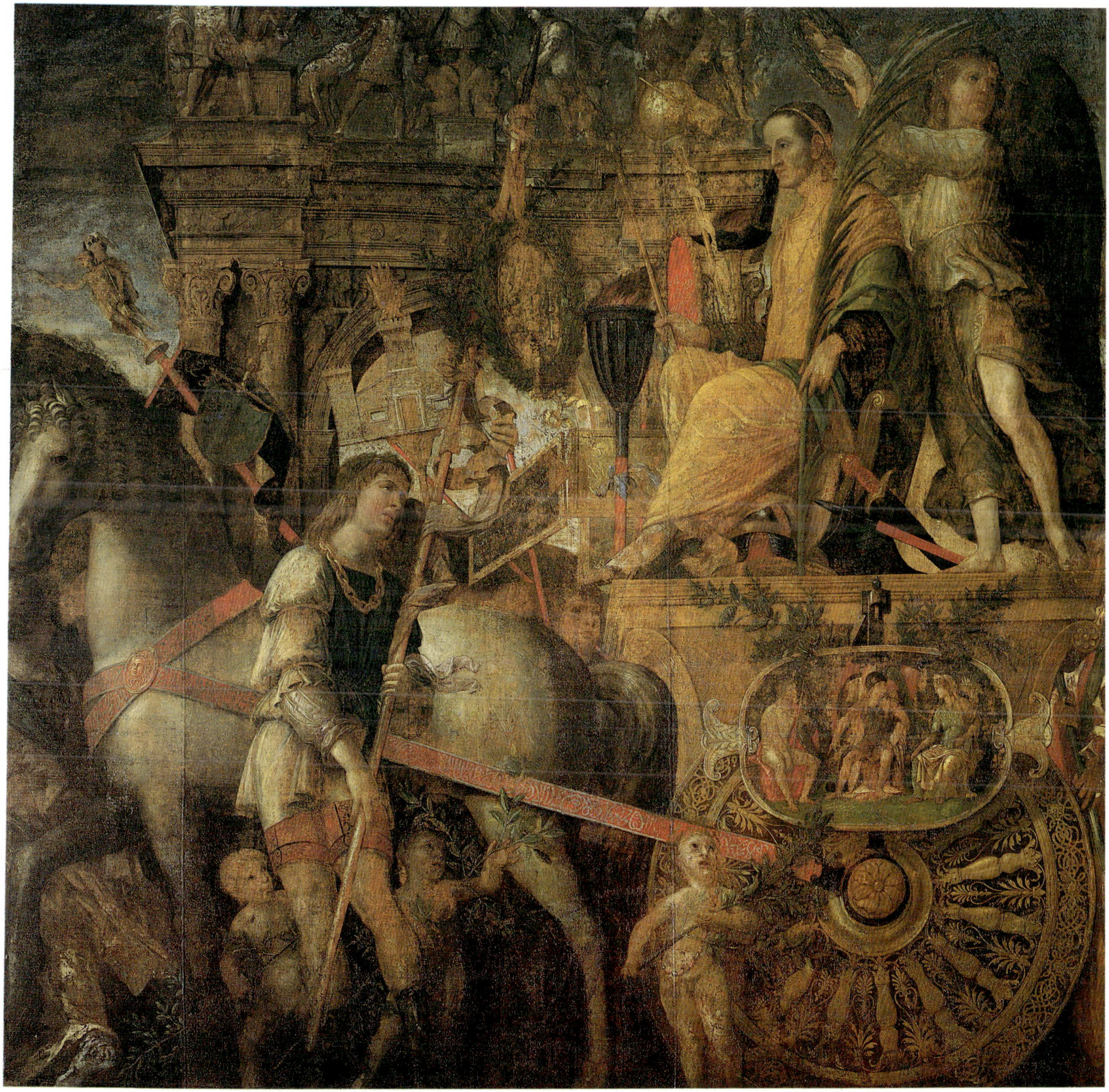

8 Julius Caesar on his triumphal chariot (*canvas IX*)